The Art of Resonant Living

Volume 1

A guide to moving from dissonance to resonance

Compiled by

Denise Harris-Heigho

Co-authors

Claire Lewis

Stefania Caria

Marian Koek

Michelle Lowe

Kristina Mendez Matejova

Joumana Nasr

Resonant Living

Media Publishing

Copyright 2016

About this book

"Create the highest, grandest vision possible for your life, because you become what you believe"

Oprah Winfrey

In life there are frequencies and balances. For some of us, life's natural ebbs and flows might seem more like monsoons and drought.

If your life, in spite of all the great things you have accomplished and wonderful people you have met along the way, feels more like the latter, **Living a Resonant Life** can help you smooth things out and lead you on a more balanced journey.

This book is part biographical, part inspirational.

Filled with real-life stories, contributed by people who have overcome obstacles and found their one true path to a happier, more fulfilling life, this book aims to inspire and empower you. No matter your circumstances, you can live the life you've always dreamed of and reignite a passion you may have lost along the way.

I would like to thank the co-authors who shared their stories showing their passion, determination and commitment to living their vision of life.

The time is now. The only thing you risk losing is more of your authentic self.

Denise Harris-Heigho

Table of Contents

"The only person you are destined to become is the person you decide to be"

Ralph Waldo Emerson

Introduction

Everything has a natural vibration. This is known as a resonant frequency and will vibrate in light of current circumstances if left unbothered. This same object will vibrate emphatically in light of vibrations of a comparable frequency near its own particular natural frequency. This wonder is called reverberation.

Living a Resonant Life is more than just feeling great. It is about finding, surrounding and living in your own natural frequency. Pierre Teilhard de Chardin said, "We are not people having an otherworldly affair. We are otherworldly people having a human ordeal". We are all spiritual creatures and in our most natural state we are of the same vibrational frequency. Through our human experience, we have forgotten who we really are and what we are capable of.

A Resonant Life is the fullest articulation of YOU – living your life in accordance with your Life purpose. Many people are already living their life purpose some of the time or in specific parts of their life already. Although in many instances individuals regularly feel like their jobs, relationships or life circumstances are keeping them from living the life they desire. In light of outside pressure and perceptions, they focus on outer sources for joy, happiness and approval to live the life they desire.

You've done the work. You've achieved what many aspire to achieve in their lifetimes. Between your job, your social life, and family obligations, your life is full – on the surface. Underneath it all, behind the façade of day-to-day pleasantries, lies something deeper – a part of you that feels unfulfilled.

You, like many others, long for a sense of purpose. You know the life you are living isn't the one you truly desire. Yes, you have the things you might need to get by, but do you have what you need to fill the void you might be feeling? Do you have a sense of self that's rooted in truth and a feeling of authenticity?

Living a Resonant Life aims to inspire you to live the life you were meant to live. Filled with poignant stories, contributed by people from all walks of life, including coaches, therapists, consultants, and entrepreneurs, this timely book shares their experiences and gives insight into how they conquered their feelings of inauthenticity. From bouts of depression, the horrors of tragedy, unfulfilling relationships, broken marriages, and career angst, each of these individuals knows what it's like to live and work through their problems and find joy on the other side by embracing a more resonant life.

Living Resonantly is a procedure of revealing what makes your heart sing and follow your internal wisdom.

My wish for you is to be able to benefit from reading stories from women from all over the world. May their tips have a beneficial effect on your life, especially for those of you who may be having or facing your own challenges. I hope you find the stories, empowering and inspiring.

Each person went on their own journey of discovery and created new more empowering outcomes. They gained inner strength, refused to give up, created positive strategies to conquer their challenges.

In most of the stories each one started from a place of not having their needs being met or being in a state of fear.

They began to want the ability to feel pleasure and joy in their lives again and reclaim their power. From this desire they found tools and techniques which helped them to increase their self- confidence, self-esteem and the ability to begin to manifest their desire.

This led them to having hope, compassion, forgiveness and were able to love themselves more.

By speaking their truth, they began to communicate their desires and listening to their inner voice.

In most cases there was a stronger knowing of their own wisdom, power of their minds and began to create the life of their inner vision.

From this came the understanding more of themselves and ability to live the life they desire on their terms. Their vibration increased significantly.

No matter what your challenges, this book can guide you on your own journey to living a more fulfilled, empowering life that speaks to who you are and where you want to be.

If you have a story you would like to share in the next volume of Resonant Living please get in touch for a chat. I would love to hear from you.

Denise Harris-Heigho

Creator and Publisher of Resonant Living Volumes

Website: www.resonantliving.co.uk
Email: denise@resonantliving.co.uk
Facebook: https://www.facebook.com/dharrisheigho
Twitter: @deharrisheigho

The Storm before the Calm

By Claire Lewis

I'd like to think my story is inspirational to anyone who is family oriented, who has or plans to have children. I hope it helps those with depression and lets them realize anything is possible.

I am no expert on this, but having suffered with depression, I feel I can reach out to some. Life is a wonderful, beautiful thing we should try to embrace the best way we can.

Before I was ready to have a baby, I decided I wanted a little girl called Mia. Mia - mine. My Mia with beautiful blue eyes just like her mummy. She would be so special. The apple of my eye.

So when I married my perfect man, Richard, we agreed we'd start trying immediately.

It took a while. Eight months to be precise. And I just thought, "Okay, that's it now. Wonderful. I'm pregnant."

I never thought about miscarriage. Five weeks later I had an extra heavy period and that was it, not pregnant anymore. I was devastated. I had been so excited and then my world had come crashing down around me.

Over the next couple of months I tried my hardest to remind myself of what lots of friends and my doctor had told me. "After a miscarriage women are particularly fertile so just keeping trying." We did and two months later I was pregnant again.

I went 7 or 8 weeks before I bled again. I sporadically bled for five weeks and I was scanned every time in the early pregnancy unit thinking I was miscarrying again. Before my first official 12-week scan I had nine scans. I was extremely anxious and frightened every time I went to the hospital, but they just kept telling me everything was fine and I could always see the heartbeat on the screen, a tiny but fast pulse which was very comforting indeed.

I'd become a huge pregnant woman very quickly. At no point was I mistaken as fat. I just looked pregnant from the start and by the second trimester the bleeding had stopped. The bigger I got, the more I could feel our baby moving around inside me. I loved being pregnant. I'd made up my own little songs which every day I'd sing to our baby whilst rubbing my tummy. "I love you baby. Everyone loves you. Life will be so wonderful." The bond I felt right from the beginning was so intense. I loved our baby so much I couldn't wait to meet the beautiful little person growing inside me.

At 20 weeks it was confirmed we were having a girl. A boy or a girl it wouldn't have mattered really. Not at all. But now all I could think was "I'm going to have my Mia" and the songs that I sang whilst rubbing my tummy changed to, "I love you Mia. Everyone loves Mia. Life will be so wonderful Mia." I loved knowing our baby girl was growing inside me and feeling her move.

Richard had a dream

The night before the scan, Richard had a dream we were going to have a girl. He woke up on the day sure that this had been some kind of premonition.

For twenty weeks we had been convinced we were having a boy due to the size of my stomach. So, when a girl was announced with conviction at the twenty-week scan and she measured on the large side, it was decided that I would be scanned again four weeks later and checked for gestational diabetes. I didn't feel like this was the case and I tested negative, although strep B was found in my blood. Bacteria harmless to adults, but to the baby during delivery possibly life-threatening. But I was told no need to worry as this was common and easily dealt with.

So with every trust in the hospital's opinion, I managed to keep calm and not stress myself over this.

I was also experiencing a lot of pain. Sharp pain deep in my stomach so lots of anxiety and worry started again. I felt in my heart something wasn't right. I knew even then that my pregnancy was by no means normal. My midwife just kept telling me that what I was experiencing was growth pain, but something just didn't feel right. My intuition was telling me otherwise.

Work, in the beginning, were pretty unsympathetic. Before I managed to get through to the owner of the business that I needed just a few allowances made due to the physicality of the job as a laser practitioner, the manager at the time was simply vile towards me. She just wouldn't give me any small extra breaks and seemed to enjoy making me feel ill and tired. So along with being stressed my back gave way, leaving me with little ability to carry out treatments effectively and professionally. The director soon rectified this problem, giving me even more leeway than I asked for. He was sympathetic, for which I was thankful, but my back had already been damaged so work continued to be a struggle.

At 31 weeks I was due to go on maternity leave and I knew from all the scans I'd had, Mia was still breech. Her head was up in my rib cage. I could feel it was still there and she hadn't turned. I remember being at work three days prior to my last day, feeling like our baby was coming. Something had changed in my pelvic area; I felt different. It felt as if my body was adjusting to being ready to go into labour.

On my last day I was having what we thought were Braxton Hicks contractions, but they were really intense, much more than they had been for the last two days. Halfway through my last day at work I just knew I needed to go to hospital. I didn't feel right at all. I was in quite a lot of pain. I was worried I was having contractions. So I made my way there and when I was finally seen, the doctor said I was having "some kind of contraction" and that they would need to keep me in overnight.

Richard came to the hospital as soon as he could and stayed with me until I seemed ready to sleep. It was no more than an hour after he had left to go home for the night that my waters broke. I was so unprepared for it. I wasn't even sure what it was. Rather than pressing the bedside buzzer for a midwife to come to me, I walked out into their office area.

"I think my waters have just broken", I said.
 I was then taken to the delivery suite where I phoned Richard, and told him, "You have to come back. Our baby is coming."

Nothing happened all night. We just sat waiting. Waiting for me to go into labour. But I didn't. The baby doctors came to see us. They were quite reassuring, although everything they said was one big blur to me. I managed to understand that 94 to 96% of babies born at 32 weeks survive. At 32 weeks the lungs are more mature and stronger than before, but to ensure this I would have a steroid injection and our baby's breathing would be assisted by oxygen once she was in the incubator, for however long was necessary.

The information was comforting, but let's face it, no amount of reassurance was going to relax me until our baby was able to come home with us.

The other piece of information I retained was something which worried me a hell of a lot. They would keep me in for a week to monitor me and if I didn't go into natural labour I would be sent home.

"What?" I thought to myself, "My baby has no water around her and I can no longer feel her moving. No that is not happening."

I just knew I would be panicking all the time with no one to come and check the heartbeat or anything. So I had a conversation with Mia, "Just hold on for a bit longer. You need to get to 32 weeks and then you can come out. We need to make sure you are strong enough, but you need to be born before the week ends."

My parents were on holiday in Italy. I just wanted my Mum. I needed as much support as I could get and my mother's affection and care were all I could think about. When I spoke to her on the phone I only needed to say it once, "I need you to come home." And straight away without hesitation, she answered, "Yes, Claire, I'm coming."

The next day my mum went to the airport in Italy, told them the situation, changed her ticket and came back to London. Just like that. And then we sat the three of us and waited. Waited and waited. Luckily the consultant decided before the week was up, I would have a C section because of the worry that the Strep B would otherwise harm the baby, but on the morning of the beginning of the 32nd week I went into natural labour. Richard and my mum came to the hospital as soon as they were notified.

The real contractions were different. They felt physically and mentally different, probably because I knew this was the real deal. They made my heart race, but I dealt with them just fine. I felt okay. I felt excited. We were about to meet our baby for the first time. Even going through to the surgery didn't really bother me. I was confident everything was going to be just fine. I had already decided and signed papers to confirm I would be taken for an emergency Caesarean if I went into labour. I could not think of anything more awful than giving birth to a breech baby. I knew I wouldn't cope with what felt like such an unusual delivery and I just wanted our baby to be ok.

 I think what was happening hit me when the local anesthetic went into my spine. I'd never thought about it, the whole of my lower body was paralysed and I felt like a two-ton weight, on top of the operating table. It was so strange to be able to move my arms and my head but nothing else. And a large blue plastic screen had gone up just below my chest so I couldn't see the operation.

At 10:39am they took Mia out and held her up for Richard and I to see her. Her mouth opened and she let out her first little scream. Relief was all I felt, but she was tiny. She was this little blob covered in blood, with extremely dark hair. Loads of hair all over her head. She was eight weeks premature after all. The baby doctors took her over to be examined just behind where I was laying and I looked over my shoulder to see Richard watching what was happening and telling me, "She's fine, she's fine." We were smiling at each other as Richard was nodding reassuringly.

Mia was 4 lbs 11 oz, which was an unbelievably positive weight for a baby born at her stage of gestation. She was taken straight to the intensive care baby unit so I didn't get to hold her which was massively upsetting. But at least I knew she was okay and I would see her very soon.

All of a sudden I felt very strange indeed. Extremely, indescribably strange. The only way I can put into words how I was feeling was that I felt sick and dizzy multiplied by 1000, laying on my back feeling nauseous to the point of choking on the nausea. Choking and panicking, my head rolling from side to side with of course still no movement in my lower body. I just remember seeing all these different faces around me, telling me to try to keep calm and Richard holding my hand, telling me the same thing but I was panic stricken. I thought I was dying.

"What's happening, what's happening?"

Was all I could keep saying, "I feel sick, I feel sick." I was so scared.

When they had tried to take out the placenta, I had hemorrhaged and lost four and a half pints of blood, just over half the human body blood composition. It felt as if all of my insides had fallen out onto the floor as I lay there scared for my life.

I was sedated and given three blood transfusions. It was confirmed that unbeknown to the hospital, during the pregnancy, I had suffered with a condition called placenta percreta, which is when the placenta embeds itself into the muscle surrounding the womb and cannot be removed normally after the baby is born.

They later described mine coming out like dead pieces of mincemeat rather than normal, whole and healthy looking like a large steak.

When I came back round again, I was on a private ward. I was groggy, I still couldn't move my legs, I was in pain and all I wanted to see was our baby. Every time I asked a nurse when I could see her, I was told they just needed to make sure I was okay first. It was made quite clear to me by the doctors that if I had given birth to Mia naturally, there wouldn't have been enough time to get me into surgery for the blood transfusions. If I had given birth naturally then I wouldn't be alive anymore. Mia being breached and the Caesarean had saved my life.

My Mia had saved my life and she knew to do that she needed to be born at 32 weeks.

I had to wait 11 hours before I could see my Mia. Eleven hours. That felt like 11 days.

Richard took me to the special care baby unit in a wheelchair. I was so excited, but I think it was then that I realized our baby was eight weeks premature. Was she really going to be okay? Was she really going to be 100% healthy? And how long would it be before she could come home? 4 lbs 11 oz for an eight weeks premature baby is a really good weight.

Mia was strong and she had been taken off the oxygen and out of the intensive care unit long before I saw her, but I didn't understand the significance of that, and the worry and anxiety just took over me. I started crying uncontrollably when I saw all the incubators and wires and machines. Our baby was tiny and I felt so naive and lost. I knew nothing about premature babies.

Everything I had been told about Mia's chances was forgotten. Every term used by the doctors when describing her condition was alien to me and I just cried my heart out. I had to sit by the door of the unit to control myself before I could see her properly but when I did something amazing happened.

She looked right at me

New born babies cannot focus their eyes properly, but the first time Mia and I saw each other she looked right at me. She looked right at me, deep into my eyes and she did every time she saw me after that. I sang to her. I sang all the few songs I'd been singing to her whilst she was in my tummy and she knew exactly who I was. Finally Mummy was here. It was an instant, powerful, inseparable connection which no amount of words can describe. But I felt it. I felt this amazing bond straight away. Every time I sang, she looked deep into my eyes.

A nurse saw us staring into each other as she was walking around the unit and she stood beside me and commented, "Wow, she knows she's yours."

The 11 hours we had waited was now forgotten and when I held Mia for the first time she crawled up into the foetal position and sat inside my top on my chest. Mia would stay like that for hours at a time. The skin to skin contact was amazing. We still do it to this day.

 But hormones must have been flying about all over the place and the trauma of what had just happened must've lodged itself in me. I couldn't stop crying. I was so worried about our baby. I realized that I would have to go home and leave her in SCBU for goodness knows how long. I kept hearing, "maybe up until her due date." Eight weeks away. I just wanted Mia to be healthy and to be able to come home. I felt so mixed up and confused. As a mother who has just given birth, your natural desire is to take your baby home with you.

Nothing the doctors told me made any sense. I felt so stupid. In my panic, I even started worrying Mia wouldn't survive. I'd got myself so worked up it was impossible for me to think straight. I was an absolute wreck. I just had to build up the courage and ask outright. It was the only way I had any hope of calming down.

I remember saying to a doctor, "I'm so so sorry I have to ask you this. Is Mia going to die?"

She was the only doctor I felt comfortable enough around to come out with the question and her sympathetic answer was "No, absolutely not. She's fine. We just have to make her strong enough so she can go home."

And so I started to understand. Mia wasn't ill, she was just small. She had jaundice and she wasn't strong enough or big enough to feed so they were feeding her through a tube to get her strength up to suck and drink milk like all babies.

Frustratingly, my milk didn't really come through either. A bit of colostrum came out so at least Mia got that, but then the amount of milk each time I pumped was so small. I was able to get 10 or 20 mls at a time when other mums around me were filling up their bottles to the brim. I think the birth caused this, but I felt so useless.

Mia had my milk, but every feed had to be topped up with formula because there just wasn't enough. I had wanted so desperately to breastfeed, but it just wasn't to be after much perseverance. It didn't feel like it at the time, but this was okay and it has made no difference to mine and Mia's relationship or to her health. Some women just cannot breast feed and the pressure to do so, is in my view unacceptable.

Four days later, I was sent home and every day from that point on I was told to rest but I couldn't. I couldn't go a single day without seeing our baby. The first night, when the time came for us to go home, it took ages for me to drag myself away from Mia.

When I did leave, it felt as if my body was leaving the hospital and my
soul was being left behind.

Every day for the next four weeks I felt this, it was agonizing. It was
unbearable. Each day I would go to the hospital to be with our
daughter. Richard would meet me there after work and each day we
would walk away because we had no choice. I felt so incomplete
without our baby. It was like living a real nightmare, but we got
through it together and at 36 gestational weeks old Mia was finally
ready to come home. She had put on two and a half whole pounds and
she was taking every feed from a bottle.

We were ecstatic. Overjoyed.

But the crying didn't stop. I was just so upset all the time and I didn't
know why. My GP surgery phoned me to book me in for an
appointment. Obviously the hospital had informed them of what had
happened and when I saw my doctor she wasn't at all surprised. She
referred me to the perinatal team at another hospital not far from our
flat. A team of doctors and nurses who look after mothers in need of
extra support and it was there, that the psychiatrist looking after me
diagnosed me with post-traumatic stress disorder.

My symptoms were a mixture of depression, I felt like I was in the
biggest, deepest, darkest hole. Anger towards everything and everyone
except our beautiful baby thank the Lord and I just couldn't accept
that there was no answer to the question in my mind all the time,
which was "Why me?" I mean the likelihood of placenta percreta
happening to anyone is extremely rare. After the delivery the surgeons
had told me they had never seen anything like it before. I just couldn't
accept it. I felt as though I would just have been better off dead. If I
had died that day, then everyone would be better off without me,
including Mia. I mean, how ludicrous.

My logical thinking, however told me to just do what I needed to do,
which was, of course, look after our baby. So I did. I did nothing
except care for Mia.

I didn't really go anywhere for the first six months. I didn't see anyone
except family. I just shut myself away from the world. I would say

actually the first 14 months of Mia's life for me, my husband and my family were a mixture of joy and pain. Whilst enduring this horrible disease I'm certain I managed to convince my husband that I didn't love him anymore. My depression made me make him feel very unwanted indeed. I suppose without realizing it, I was very unaffectionate and pretty cold towards him.

We have struggled through it together, trying our absolute hardest to give Mia an amazing life so she would never realize the extent of our heartache.

I have had countless amounts of extremely helpful therapy sessions and I am still on medication. I have no plans to come off it yet, but I am confident that I am so near the end of all this. I'm now able to realize I am getting better and when I have a bad day I can tell myself that the feeling of darkness will pass.

I think time is a massive part of the healing process. Mia is 18 months now and she is wonderful. She makes me and my husband very proud to be parents. Mia is bright, alert, and intelligent.

She loves books being read to her and when we talk to her, she understands every word and copies some of what we say. She is such a happy child and she is strong minded. So many people used to tell me, "she is calm and happy because of you" and I never believed them but now I am confident they were and still are completely correct. Everywhere I go people comment on Mia's beautiful little face, her curly hair, and how well behaved she is.

I'm a good mum and I know it. I've made myself focus on the positives. The question is no longer, "why me?", it's "well, why not me?" I'm strong enough.

My mind was at war with my body

My mind was at war with my body, but I have forgiven my body now. I accept that it happened to me and to us.

Despite all my doubt I was always going to come out the other side absolutely fine. Writing this too has been excellent therapy.

I have a wonderful husband and I am certain when I tell him I will never stop loving him, he believes me. I will never be able to thank my family enough for all their support, and my mum? I've always said she's like my guardian angel. And finally our daughter is an absolute godsend. I never realized how happy she was always going to make me. I smile every day. We laugh together all the time.

Our love for each other is unconditional and when she is old enough, I will tell her she saved my life. But also that we did it together. Together we made sure that everything would be okay in the end. I adore her and my life as her mother and it is that has made me get better. And has she got blue eyes just like her mummy? Of course she has. Pretty rare too for a mixed race child.

Always try to remember these five things. They helped me tremendously: -

1. Focus on what/who you love. Find someone or something you can put your strength into. It sounds cliché but love makes us strong.

2. Find someone you can talk to. Whether it is a family member, friend, or medical professional, talking really does help.

3. Don't be ashamed to take medication, alternative or otherwise. Depression is a disease and should be treated that way. Find what works for you and believe that one day that chemical change in your brain will happen and you will be happy again. It just takes time.

4. Write everything down. Your thoughts. Your highs and your lows. Keeping a diary is an excellent option.

5. Remember the happy days will start to outnumber the sad. When you are down, tell yourself that you know very soon you will be okay again

Change is a curve. If a change happens in your life, it will affect how you feel. At various stages you might feel curious or bored, angry, in or out of control or overwhelmed, excited, relieved, nervous or strong. Much of this depends on what's changing, on how much you can control it and what's in it for you.

Try to believe in yourself as much as you can.

I'd like to thank firstly of course, my husband for his honest and eternal love. I know the whole ordeal has been hard, but we got through it together. We know nothing will break us.

My parents for their help and support literally at the drop of a hat. Whenever I was upset or needed help they were there by my side.

Other family members. As my brother in his own way without probably even realizing, has been an excellent listener. Denise Harris Heigho for cousin in law/sisterly support NLP business and personal development Coach. She helped my inner strength come back. And Auntie Monica, who is like a Mum to Richard and so makes a wonderful mother in law for me.

All the staff at the Homerton Hospital SCBU. Their care for Mia was trusted the whole time she was there. In particular a nurse called Michelle. She was fantastic, emotional support to me whenever she was on duty.

Dr Rebecca Moore and Kate Tangri, perinatal team at Mile End Hospital for really getting to the bottom of and ending the depression which I felt was never going to go away.

Close friends Lisa, Maral and Roxie for being there for me and tolerating my worst moods.

And finally, Mia when you are old enough to understand I will tell you how you saved my life and made it complete.

About Claire Lewis

Claire Lewis is a BeautyTherapist / Aesthetician

Location: London, UK

Contact: www.enhanceyou.co.uk

Notes & Ideas:

"Progress is Impossible without Change
and those who cannot

change their minds

cannot change anything"

George Bernard Shaw

LOVE AND FREEDOM

By Stefania Caria

Be the director of your life.

When I was 13, I decided to undertake humanistic studies to avoid maths as much as possible as I am convinced that I have an allergy to numbers!

I decided that I would rather spend hours translating ancient texts from Latin and Greek and carry heavy dictionaries to school rather than solving maths problems. In my third year of secondary school, I had my first encounter with Philosophy. The word philosophy comes from the Greek, and it means love of knowledge. Isn't it fascinating?

I still clearly remember that evening, when I read the introduction to my philosophy manual[1]: five minutes of intellectual bliss.

It was my first life insight: powerful, profoundly meaningful and intense like thunder rumbling in a dark sky. It made me tremble and in a fraction of a second showed me the way out from the darkness.

It was so profound that I felt emotional and warm tears crossed my cheeks. It was a sweet, cathartic and liberating cry. From that precise moment I knew what I wanted to do and I knew that the understanding and study of human behaviour would become my focus for the rest of my life.

I completed my humanistic studies and then went to study Psychology, specializing in Occupational Psychology. University was a fascinating and intellectual adventure: five years studying what I loved most and was passionate about.

My ego was comfortable and flattered by good grades and lots of recognition from my parents and friends. After graduating, I worked

---

[1] Reale, D. – Antiseri, D. 1990. Manuale di Filosofia. Brescia: Editrice La Scuola.

and similarly produced good results, but I got too comfortable, and I needed a new scenario, new challenges, and perspective.

For three months, Stockholm became my new scenario. It was my first time abroad, and how I would understand later, it was a point of no return. When I came back to Italy and my city, I could not help but feel alienated and it was impossible to be the same person I was, before leaving. Being exposed to a foreign reality opened my mind and made me feel alive and mentally stimulated. This discovery of a different world and its attached sensations caused an irreversible change in the way I relate to others. When I came back to Italy I was missing that stimulation and struggling to fit in as reality seemed flat and not in line with my new perspective.

I wanted to feel on the edge, and there is not a better way to do it than living in a foreign country without speaking the local language. I understand that it does not sound wise to move abroad without having learnt the language, but I could not wait any longer. I had to leave because I felt that my time in Italy was up and felt that taking extra time to improve my English was not an option. I thought that you only learn the language from real life and not from a lesson or a book. In addition to this I really needed to give myself a life challenge to understand who I really was and what I could achieve starting from scratch. As I said earlier, I could not adjust back to the limited reality of my city, but I wanted to keep learning and 'feel uncomfortable'. In light of this new approach to life, I decided to move abroad and as I wanted to learn English and experience a diverse environment, I chose London.

I left my professional job and moved there to earn £5.50 per hour. Was I brave or was I crazy? Certainly desperate and ignorant about minimum wage! I was making enough money to survive, but this did not make me feel devalued or depressed, on the contrary, I felt very much alive. I did not feel as if I was going back in my life, but I felt I was going forward. It was an incredible experience!

What made it incredible was that feeling of continuous learning and exploration necessary to survive.

It was exciting and stimulating, even if there was a huge side effect waiting for me.

Anxiety trap

Imagine someone like myself who values, knowledge and intellect as her only way to be. Imagine a person who seeks and gain attention through her intelligence and the ability to express this through language. Try and take this away from this person, what is left?

The answer for me was: panic.

Even if the whole experience of living in a foreign country was electrifying, there was still a part of me suffering because people thought I was stupid or slow and I was struggling to express myself. This made me feel like losing part of my personality.

I knew it was a temporary loss. I was learning and stretching myself, and it felt great to fight for a better future. This is a battle that many people choose to join all over the world. Being a foreign person is not easy and often the language barrier is so thick that it confines people into menial jobs.

Many do work long hours for a little pay, and they don't get the chance to improve their language skills because their colleagues are from the same country or speak the same language. At the same time, it is difficult to find a good job if you don't speak the national language and it becomes a vicious circle difficult to break.

Despite my ups and downs, my passion and drive got me going until I achieved what I wanted. Within a year, I was able to learn English to an advanced level and moved from the scenario of 'shaking because my phone is ringing I won't understand a word' to working as a Careers Adviser at a small college. Yes! That was pretty good, and I was satisfied with my results.

However, it only felt good for a short while. I recognized that I started from zero and progressed to a certain level, which from a rational point of view was an excellent result. However, only part of me was satisfied with the results. The other part of me thought it was not good enough because I wanted to be perfect and even my advanced level of English was not sufficient because I wanted to speak and write like a native speaker.

What would I be if I could not be intellectual and articulate? This was a terrifying encounter with anxiety.

It hit me so hard that it penetrated every cell of my body. I was not able to sleep, think, enjoy life and most importantly be. It was a generalised and yet stabbing feeling that made me hopeless like an animal caught in a trap. I felt like a victim who did not even had the strength to scream. It was like sipping a toxic poison that started to paralyse every area of my life to the point that I fell ill.

I developed chronic dizziness.

I had to stop working for four months and go back to Italy.

The solution was in the pain

I now think that those four months of illness were the solution. In other words, through my disease, I created the mental space to allow a meaningful insight which healed my anxiety.

This was the second most valuable insight into my life after the 'philosophy moment' I described earlier in this chapter.

As I have explained, the only way I could express myself and feel recognized was through intellectual performance. For the first time, I was not producing, working, making money or studying... I was not doing anything.

I was just ill.

At that point an important realisation started to emerge from the bottom of my heart: those who loved me kept loving me regardless of what I was doing or producing and most importantly regardless the results I was achieving. This simple realisation made me understand the self-limiting belief underlying my health issue: 'To be loved, I have to be good at whatever I do'.

This belief was the source of my anxiety.

I also realised that I was not just applying this belief to others, but I was imposing this condition to myself. I could not love myself unless I was performing and achieving. As a result, I did not love myself unconditionally and constantly needed others to tell me who I was. I needed people to validate me and fill that emotional void I had inside.

We all know on a rational level that to love others, you must love yourself first. It is common knowledge, but it has not been easy to understand, internalise and embody this simple truth at a deeper emotional level.

It took me a long time.

This realisation also helped me reevaluate my intellectual nature. Understanding the way I used this personal characteristic to draw attention and being loved, made me realise that I could just enjoy being intellectual without having a second reason. I could finally benefit from the positive elements of possessing or showing intellect or mental capacity without expecting something in exchange. This is important because when you do things to get something in return sooner or later you will be in trouble.

I know it is not easy, but life sometimes gives you just what you need in that precise moment and it gave me the opportunity to break that belief by making me ill and unproductive. My illness was my chance to understand that life is not a box ticking exercise and that you don't have to achieve anything to prove your value and be loved. The only thing that life wants you to do is to be.

Be your whole self.

Overcoming barriers

Being your whole self will also help you overcome any type of barriers. In my experience, it has been challenging to learn a new language and survive in a foreign country. However, I was not ready to be stopped by a language barrier and was firmly determined to break it down and succeed. I had the strong internal belief that I would find a way to get there, no matter what.

So, it did not matter if:

-   People treated me unfairly or tried to humiliate me.

-   I lost my professional status and had to start from scratch

- I could not express my thoughts or understand what people told me

If you believe in yourself and hold on tight to your personal confidence you will find a way forward and have the courage to make the changes to bring about happiness and success. Instead, if you don't believe in your value and abilities you will never even try and succeed. You will feel stuck in the trap you have created for yourself.

In life, you can stand in two positions: you can be at the cause or on the effect side of your life.

Being on the effect side of your life is all about making excuses and finding reasons why you can't have the life you want. In this position you end up blaming everything and everyone: the government, the economy, your boss, your partner, etc. It is quite an exhaustive job which can drain a lot of energy out of you and can make you angry, bitter and depressed.

And what do you achieve? An extensive list of excuses.

The opposite of excuses is results and to get results you would need to move away from the EFFECT side and shift towards CAUSE.

'Being at cause is all about choosing to do what you want to do and when you want to do it.' Rather than making excuses, you can invest your energy into getting results in your life. You can choose which jobs you want, which relationship you want to be in, which state of mind you want to experience.

Ultimately, you can choose your life.

How would it be if you learnt how to be at cause in your life and not let other people's behaviour affect you?

You will stop saying things like: 'he or she makes me depressed' or 'she is driving me mental,' 'this job makes me miserable' the truth is no one has control over how you feel, except yourself. So the real question is: 'How his or her behaviour is making you choose to feel depressed'?

Being aware that you can make this shift in your mind and that you can choose to be at cause and being in control of your emotional states, will have a tremendous effect on your self-confidence and the ability to steer your life in the right direction.

You can choose to claim your power back if you feel that you have been robbed by someone or an event of your life. You just need to embrace this empowering principle and keep focusing on what you have, what you want while moving your focus away from what you don't have and don't want.

Focusing on what you don't have, thinking about the sacrifices that you have to make and feeling sorry for your life might get you some momentary and fleeting compassion but won't make you move forward, not even an inch. I explore this topic in greater detail in my book 'Travelling within. Destination Self-Love'

So...what is stopping you now from achieving what you want? Remember, no one has the right to stop you in your journey toward success and fulfillment, not even yourself. This empowering belief will make you a true winner in every situation.

It is impossible to run out of love

In your journey through the obstacles of life remember to be love.

We tend to think that love is an object that can be exchanged for something else and if you love and don't receive anything back, your love will be lost.

You cannot lose love once you have given it away. Like knowledge, you need to have it first before sharing it. After teaching others, you will see that you still have the same amount of knowledge, if not more. In the same way, you need to have love in you before giving it to others and it won't be lost even if given to thousands.

Loving oneself does not mean being narcisisstic or tell yourself you are beautiful when you reflect your image in a mirror or take selfies. Loving oneself is the basis of love and it is a genuine interest, care and respect for your individuality. It is recognising that you are unique and getting excited about what you are and what you can become.

The idea of what you can become and seeing yourself as infinite possibility should be enough to make you feel instantly excited. This never ends because your potential does not run out, no matter how old you are. The more you fulfill your potential, the more you feel compelled to continue and develop yourself.

'Love and the self are one and the discovery of either is the realisation of both'[2]

Once you love yourself, you can then love others and the universe. Please note that universal love is not romantic love, which is just a fraction of the powerful love you can experience in life. Loving others is a great source of joy and while I have described anxiety as a toxic poison, love is a warm light that radiates from your heart and revitalises every cell of your body while caressing your soul.

Once you have discovered this, you are no longer at the mercy of external forces as you have acquired the most powerful force in life.

As the Latin idiom says: Amor Vincit (love conquers all)

Please remember that discovering love does not mean having an internal energy that lies dormant within you and awaits a special and mystical moment to be awakened. As you learn to be a human being, in the same way, you learn to discover love.

Love education

In my life experience I have noticed that we tend to accept the idea of love uncritically. We all think that love is important and that we must experience it and this makes many of us frantically looking for it.

Do we ever spend time doubting and pondering love? Is love all there is? Would it not be rather simple? If love is so central in our lives, should we not spend more time studying it, understanding and learning about it? And once we understand enough about love should we not share this learning with others?

No one teaches you about love even if we are desperate to learn.

---

[2] Buscaglia, B. 1972. Love. Toronto: Ballantine Books

This is important to me because there is a lot of loneliness, suffering and confusion among human beings that comes from this mysterious idea of love. Society thinks that love is simply getting married, having children and providing for your family. We also think that once you have ticked those boxes that will provide enough evidence for yourself and others that you are lovable and you fit in. Is that real? Is love just that?

I think that most of us are lost and know that the idea of 'love education' might sound a little strange, but if you reflect for a second, you will understand the importance of it.

If you wanted to become a chef, you would study the art of cooking and spend a lot of time practising so that you would develop expertise and then share what you know. After you have learnt, you would guide others and make them feel confident.

Why should it be different for learning the art of love?

'To study love, you must live in love and ultimately BE LOVE'.[3]

Everyone has a limitless potential to love and be loved, but potential requires work to be realised and developed.

Through this chapter you had the opportunity to acquire the awareness of the greatest strength: LOVE.

As a result of this new understanding, you will stop seeking love frantically because you will realise that love is not something to be found but it is everywhere. To look for love means deceiving yourself.

Seeing and feeling love everywhere is one of the most ecstatic feelings you could ever experience in life, it will free you from fear which is the source of all negative emotions.

You will do that by releasing your negative emotions and consequently learn to heal the wounds that kept you paralyzed and finally open your heart to welcome the ultimate form of love.

This will have a positive effect on people around you, and it will also have a wonderful reflection on your business, relationships, health

---

[3] Buscaglia, B. 1972. Love. Toronto: Ballantine Books

and overall happiness. And if you feel that changes are required in your life don't feel guilty or depressed, but simply be willing to do some work.

Living and growing in love as opposed to looking for love requires courage, being real and human.

To spread love to everyone and everything, you will need to bridge the gap created by the artificial society which sees universal love as a romantic weakness. Society feels much more comfortable if you reserve love for special people in special occasions, rather than giving it to everyone.

I am aware that it is challenging to embrace real love when you are walking through cruelty, degradation, misery, selfishness and exploitation. However, if you rely on the external world to reinforce your loving instinct, you will soon be disappointed. You must have strength and plant love in your inner soul in a way that nothing and no one can pull it out. You will still be able to see evil and hate, but when you have love inside, you will recognise this as a higher force and will be able to fight doubt and confusion. It will give you strength, independence and freedom and you won't need anyone to reinforce or validate yourself.

One of your deepest fears might be that if you open yourself to love you will be vulnerable, but as I said earlier real love including love for yourself does not make you weak.

It takes courage, but it will make you stronger in the long term.

Also, remember to love because you will, as Buddha says:

'Flowers bloom because they must, not because people are fawning over them. You live and love because you will and because you want.'

I met many women whose life has been damaged by abuse which was under the guise of love. I am not talking about women with low self – esteem and low education, but individuals with super traits like empathy, helpfulness and trust. Sadly, one of the reasons why these women were targeted and victims of evil acts was represented by these 'super qualities' they had.

So now you might think that they embraced love, this then clouded their judgement, they were vulnerable and for this reason it is not such a great idea to open your heart to love.

The same women who survived the most terrifying 'emotional rapes' understood that what happened to them did not have anything to do with love or loving themselves. The reality is that was that a pathological behaviour was inflicted on them and they just did not know enough to be able to recognise the danger.

Despite the trauma, many of these women survived and decided that life and happiness is worth fighting for. Step by step they forgave themselves, constantly worked on their bleeding heart with care and kindness, day after day, month after month until one day they started smiling again.

Every loving smile brought them closer and closer to authentic love and they are now living an authentic life.

Isn't real love worth the courage and the effort?

My path towards love went through illness and lead to the realisation that there are no requirements to be loved. To love yourself, you don't have to pass an exam every day, you don't have to prove anything to anyone or meet any criteria or conditions. You just need to be who you are. You don't even need to get ill to reach this insight. The only reason why I had to go through the pain is because I was resisting my own self and reality and did not have the courage to open my eyes and look at what was wrong. Sometimes it seems easier to be blind, but it is worth facing those fears that are holding you back from being happy and real. The secret lies in listening to yourself and create the mental space to let your inner voice emerge from the bottom of your soul. This is your opportunity to listen to it, understand who you really are and become what you want to be. Love will guide you through this journey and allow you to realise yourself while bringing authenticity to your life.

These are five things I have learned and would like you to remember:

1. Be at cause in your life and invest your energy in achieving what you want.

2. Don't let anything stop you, but use obstacles and challenges as opportunities to grow

3. Recognise your self-worth: you are the most important person in your life.

4. Be resilient and bounce back when things don't go as planned.

5. Don't look for love, but be love.

And if your life is not filled with love right now, remember you can repair and rebuild. It does not matter how long it will take you, as long as you don't stop believing in the healing power of real love.

Open your heart to love and get ready to celebrate your new life!

"To Love oneself

Is the beginning

Of a lifelong romance"

Oscar Wilde

About Stefania Caria

Stefania Caria is an author, NLP practitioner, coach, Reiki Master and founder of verusvita.com.

She is also a Career Consultant, a Hypnotherapist and Time Line therapist. Stefania is passionate about self-empowering and continuous personal growth. Helping people who want to develop self-awareness and take control and live authentic and ecstatic lives.

Website: www.verusvita.com

Location: London, UK

Notes & Ideas:

"New beginnings are often disguised as painful endings"

Lao Tzu

What's Buddhism gotta do with it?

By Marian Koek

I have had a business for about 14 years. As a freelance certified pubic accountant, I mainly sell my hours to governmental services and NGO's. And my job was running well, but I had to put many hours in, because I always overloaded myself. The fear of not having enough work controlled me and I felt I could never reject a new client or job. But the last couple of years I got tired and I thought, OK, there must be another way to make money and to be happy in my business.

In my corporate life I'm an accountant and in my private life I am a Buddhist.

Buddhism is a way of living for me: it is all based on the philosophy that the Buddha is to be found in everybody. And that I am responsible for every choice I make in my life, even my attitude.

You just have to tap into the 3 characteristics of the Buddha within you: wisdom, compassion and courage. So that can help you to overcome struggles in your life. And I do that by meditation, study, reflection and sharing my experiences with others.

Although I was using Buddhist principles in my business, I never wanted to talk about this with my clients. I came to the conclusion that I was not going to hide this anymore, because I cannot separate this anymore. Buddhism is my life.

Part of Buddhism is that you share your experiences, but I never wanted to share my experiences how I use Buddhism in business. I thought people would judge me because being a spiritual accountant is something that may be looked at in a different way. I thought I might lose clients if I would share this. So I only told clients or co-workers when I felt comfortable to do so. But that was of course my own limiting belief.

So after so many years working so many hours, I felt tired and I wanted to transform my business into SMART working and more free time to travel. Also the fact that my partner got sick made me realize that I should make more time to enjoy things together. That meant that I had to choose a different business model: from selling hours to selling products.

I made the BIZZ Road Map, especially to empower women entrepreneurs to grow, in 10 steps. By transforming my own business I can help women entrepreneurs transform their business with a different mindset & focus, leading to growth and more freedom. And to be happier entrepreneurs!

But it was not always like this.

The reason I started my own company was because I had issues working in companies. I had a sharp mind and was quick in understanding the problems and solutions. But I was kept short many times, so I could not grow as fast as I wanted. I was fed up with not being able to grow, fed up that people felt threatened by my existence.

At the time I was working in Aruba I had a problem with my manager and it came to the legal issue. After that I came to the conclusion it's not about money and it's not about status. It's all about doing the work that you love.

Well the thing is that I do believe that things like that happen when there are also other issues in your life. It's just like Murphy's Law. One thing happens and then another thing happens. My mother got sick and she got lung cancer. When that happened, I had to travel to the Netherlands a lot, so my manager in Aruba thought it was a good idea to send me back to the Netherlands. But I didn't want to be sent back. They tried to find ways to prove I was not good in my work to get rid of me that way. I was an accountant and my manager had no title, so I guess he felt threatened. I think also that business was not going that great so he saw an opportunity to get rid of an expensive expat. And he used my mother's health situation. He did not count on me to fight back and thought this was the best solution for everybody.

Unfortunately, it led to a court case. And of course it was not the right time because my mother was very sick. What seemed at that time a horrible thing – I was sent back to Holland – was a great thing because I was able to spend time with my mother who was dying. So it was really a great benefit that I got out of this negative situation: I had the chance to go and stay with my mother more than a month. But the whole situation drained me and I thought: "How am I going to get out of this situation? What am I going to do? What effect will this have on my career?" I started doubting myself, doubting that I wasn't a good accountant or wouldn't be appreciated as one. So a lot of doubt surfaced.

My ex colleague's brother was a lawyer and he helped me. The court case lead to a settlement and I could go back to Aruba. So yes, you can say that the universe did deliver a solution.

And I knew there was a job in Aruba to go back to, but with a lot less salary and less benefits.

Help was being offered right away. As a Buddhist I know now (I was not a Buddhist at that moment) that I must have made some good causes in my life because after my job situation in Aruba a client helped me and they hired me right away. So I started working with them right away, first as a volunteer and after the court case they put me on their payroll.

This experience in Aruba made me realize that the job I had been working in was not for me. I was happy to have left the rat race: working long, long hours, draining energy and unhappy people working there. The universe once again took care of that and gave me a job that I could contribute something to the society in Aruba. It was an NGO that hired me and it was the first job I could combine my two professions: work as an accountant helping the co-workers budget their projects and as a teacher helping Aruban high school students with their homework in Dutch. What great benefit I got out of losing my high paid job! And this paved my way to help more NGO's in the future.

A traumatic divorce led to growth.

When I came to Aruba I was out of harmony after a tough divorce. I was trying to find myself and that was the reason I went to Aruba in the first place. My divorce was a traumatic experience. It was very hard to deal with. I was put down so much in my marriage. And I had never lived alone. So I challenged myself and wanted to prove that I could stretch my limits and make it anywhere. So I saw a job in Aruba and went for it. I left Holland and went to live in Aruba - coming out of my comfort zone - to be able to reflect and start a new life.

The interesting part is that my ex-husband was in a way jealous of my title too (like my ex-manager in Aruba). We had a house together and when I left the house we had to divide everything. He made a whole list of everything and what the actual value was. So we could divide it by value. He thought he was entitled to get a bigger part of the house because I spent a lot of time studying while he worked in the house. And he wanted to get the benefits of me being a CPA now, because he would never enjoy them due to our divorce.

The court case due to the issues I had with the manager in Aruba changed everything and led me into another direction. At first I thought my career was destroyed, like the relationship with my ex-husband. But then I saw new opportunities.

After I went back to Holland (my own choice), I went to work for a different company as an advisor. I discovered there I was good at sales and then I decided that I would start my own company.

After my mother's death and the court case I encountered Nichiren Daishonin's Buddhism. That gave me the strength and determination to continue. I went back to Aruba with the determination that nobody ever was going to put me down again or decide what I can or cannot do.

I discovered I had a big reservoir of strengths, like determination and the ability to rely on my education and title. Knowing that I could work anywhere. That nobody could ruin my career. So I let go of the career I started working in when I studied and I found my own way to be successful.

Tools and techniques I used to get through

I found the greatest tool of all: Nichiren Buddhism. I don't think that I would have ever started my own company if I hadn't been a Buddhist. Faith in myself: to trust myself that there's always a solution and I can create whatever I want to create. I'm responsible for everything that I think, say and do. I cannot blame anybody for my own unhappiness. Those are the tools that I still use.

When I don't use those tools I really feel it in my energy levels. So if I don't practice Buddhism, I feel it right away. I get into problems or I don't feel strong enough. I feel weak, drained, so it's all about using the tools. And it helps me also to put responsibility where it belongs. Not to put everything on my own plate. I can now easily say to somebody: "It's not my responsibility, but yours". And I put it on the plate of somebody else, where it belongs. I do this in my private life and by the way it's also done to me in my private life. And I also do this in my business.

In business it helps to say it's not my responsibility. I'm not putting it on my plate. Somebody else has to solve this. Knowing what's yours and what somebody else's, makes life a lot easier.

5 steps that help you to get out from where you are to back in place

I take 5 steps that I have learned through my experiences to overcome challenges. I would like to share them with you:

Step 1: Raise your energy level.

The first most important step is to raise your energy level. I do this by practising Buddhism, but you can also do it by meditation or prayers or affirmations or yoga or whatever works for you. This will help you cope with your challenges better.

Step two: Trust your wisdom.

You have a lot of wisdom. Don't listen to people who are telling you different and never achieved what you want to achieve. When you meditate, you go inside of yourself. So that's how this step connects to step number one. You connect with your own wisdom and that will help you to make the right decisions.

Step three: Create your own solution.

Never, ever give up on your own passion. Listen to yourself. Don't let anybody put you down. There's always a solution and you can create the solution. It's not depending on anybody or just circumstances. So that is really my life lesson.

Step four: Ask for help.

Educate yourself, read books, go to courses, follow trainings. Surround yourself with positive people. And find a coach or somebody, a mediator, that helps you look. They are the mirror to look in a different way to your problems. That helps you to see things clearer so you can grow.

Step five: Take action!

Listen to your own wisdom and then take action. A lot of people don't take the last step. They have wisdom and the knowledge. They have intuition. They have read all those books and have gone to a lot of courses. They go to coaches. They educate themselves, but they don't take action. Don't sit at home and sit on the couch and think, "Oh no, I did this and I did this and now I wait and everything is going to change." It's not going to change. You have to take steps if you want change. You need to take action to make the changes!

About the author

Marian Koek is the creator of the Creating Value Cards, based on the "BIZZ Road Map": in 10 steps to working smarter, more balance and better results in your business.

Since 1997 she has been a practitioner of Nichiren's Buddhism and she uses practical Buddhist principles to stand in her power as an entrepreneur.

Marian combines the rational world of the solution oriented accountant with the intuitive world of the Buddhist, who overcomes challenges with wisdom and by taking action.

She believes that if you follow your passion and use your talents, the rest will follow: better results and contentment.

In this way she helps other female entrepreneurs to make a difference in the world, to achieve their goals and to become happier entrepreneurs.

Website: www.bizzroadmap.com

Location: De Haag, Holland

Notes & Ideas:

The Truth About Love & Disappointment
By Michelle Lowe

Deciding to leave my marriage was one of the toughest challenges I have endured in my life. What made me decide to leave is I became extremely unhappy and unhappiness is one word, which is not in my vocabulary. If I were to describe to you, which colour the word "unhappy" felt like, the colour would be black. Or to be clear, I felt as though I was in a dark place. People often asked me how I reacted at the time of my decision. I explained how I tried to work through the problems, I tried to see reason and I tried to get my spouse to meet me half way. I was really sad and tried to talk through our issues, but he was not open to communicating with me in any way.

It physically affected me, soon I became unwell, I constantly had knots in my stomach, I was unable to exercise, I wasn't able to sleep well at all, I wasn't eating, in general I wasn't able to concentrate at work either.

It affected my emotions deeply and I was so stressed out all the time, probably anxious. None of the above, were necessarily obvious to me at the time, but you know looking back, I can say that I was sometimes scared of what I got myself into and I was angry and disappointed. I became lethargic and started to lose my hair. I don't mind sharing with you that the person that I was before the relationship and the person I became in, during and after the relationship differed and thus, it really led me to a dark place.

I loved being a caretaker, I wanted to be a mother and it didn't really happen in the traditional sense. I am still very motherly in relationships towards people and if I care about you and I love you, I like to take care of you. So I was very kind, very open, happy, warm fun loving. I liked myself, I was a good person and very popular. I have never been someone who has tried to fit in. I have always been

someone who wanted to just be who I am, and when I no
longer recognized who I was, that's when the change happened.

When I noticed I was no longer the person I truly loved to be is when I
made the decision that I wanted to go back to being who I truly am.
Becoming invisible in the marriage, was one thing, but I also started to
lose who I was which was way more important than any relationship I
could be in.

I was so unhappy

Invisibility was absolutely not okay with me. I took the first steps to
reclaiming me. One thing that was most important in the first step
was recognizing that I had lost who I was. It was the awareness,
because often you are in denial that something is going on however, I
couldn't deny it because I was physically seeing the change in the way
my body now looked and also in the person I was becoming. I didn't
even recognize who I was. I was so unhappy, and as I said before,
unhappy is not part of my vocabulary, so I knew something was off
and that I had to make a change.

Our relationship was falling apart like a set of dominos and
consequently it affected my relationship with my friends and family,
but to be clear, I began to sound and feel like a broken record. I began
to feel like the "friend" that everyone has, who, when they call you and
they want to see you, you begin to cringe because you are already
thinking "here we go again". I have to hear the woe is me story for the
15th time, or the "you don't know how bad my life is!"

In order to find a solution to the challenges I was experiencing, my
first decision happened when I chose to go and have therapy. It's quite
interesting actually, as a friend of mine said you know if you are so
unhappy sometimes it's just better to talk to a third party. I thought
that's great I shan't burden my friends and family - let me talk to
someone else.

You know exactly what to do

At my appointment the therapist said to me "... so here is the issue you
have Michelle, you know exactly what to do, you are just not doing it

and I could sit here and take your money and I am happy to do so if you want me to, however, . . . You have already told me what you need to do, so you just have to do it" and that was kind of eye opening for me. I told myself, "okay, so much for my therapy"!

After my conversation with the therapist the second step I took was to qualifying the decisions I was about to make and to ensure they were real and not based on peer pressure. When I say peer pressure, not what my family and friends were saying not just my inner voice, but sort of qualifying the situation was real.

For example, once I told my ex-husband, "I'm really not happy, this is really not working and I am really going to leave you, if you are not willing to make xyz changes or talk to me about making the changes or working with me on making the changes." But he would just brush me off he essentially said, "you would never leave me, you love me too much." I guess he wanted to test his theory? So we did!

With all the questions and qualifiers - I was still getting the same answers. Instead of having that dialogue with myself in my head, I was having the dialogue with him asking the same questions I had been asking myself giving myself the answers. However, I was not giving him the opportunity to answer them and the sad thing was everything that I had asked in my head, was what he had answered by just not answering. Showing me that he either didn't care or didn't want to be bothered to do the work to make things right. So looking back, that was the main thing that I did, it was the third step.

 The first approach was therapy the second was talking, but there were other steps I needed to take in order to remain true to myself in order to get through this time step by step to find a solution.

I had to figure out how to stay and get through this transition. Once I started talking to my husband, I was able to confirm my decision was right. Deciding what the next step would be, which wasn't easy, of course, but in the end I trusted my good old faithful intuition.

My intuition has never let me down and I was sort of ignoring it. I was focused on my marriage vows to which I had been committed. I had to live up to them and follow through and divorce was not a solution, certainly not an option for me. I had to work through it. But I realized whether it was an option or a solution for me, if the other person isn't on the same page, it doesn't matter what you think or feel. If you are in a one-person relationship and a relationship is a partnership that is really not a one-person situation.

I was in a dark place

That is exactly where we were, somewhat mentally divorced anyway. We had already moved on. He was very resentful and I just felt as though I wanted to stick to my decision. I had to be sure that if I walked away, I needed to be completely and utterly confirmed about it, that I had done everything that I could have done to solve and salvage our marriage.

I asked him to do therapy - he refused, I asked him to talk to family members - he refused. Or even to perhaps just have a third party interject who could be objective about our perspectives. But he refused and moved into another bedroom. So there was no marital sex happening. He would come in and not speak to me. I would ponder and say to myself "wow, if I am paying all the bills, managing the household and acting like the glue to keep us together, then why am I living this solitary life within a marriage? Then why I am I married?"

As I said earlier, I was in a dark place, I had to figure out a way to get out. I must admit I think I did a lot of things that may have not helped but I spent less time at home, I spent less time in his space, just so that I would not feel the thick atmosphere that was around us that you could cut with a knife.

I began to do things that made Me happy

As a consequence of spending less time at home and more time with friends and myself, I began to do things that made **me** happy. I began the initial steps of trying to reconnect with myself. When you are in a marriage, you still need to be an individual. Even if unconsciously, you end up giving up something that gives balance in a relationship you know it can't be all about what you want, or what they want to make it work. You want to come together, so you compromise. I quickly realized that I had compromised pretty much everything I had.

I would go to brunch with the girls on Sundays. I would do my nails, although that was not really doing my own thing. It was finding sanity outside of a marriage that is not working.

At work I had tough manager and that relationship was no longer working either. I tried to make sense of the ensuing madness by going dancing and that helped to ease the pain.

I tried to go to yoga, but it wasn't really working. It was inconsistent due to the long hours I was working. I couldn't go dancing at night due to late night events. I could go off to work and hide but even that became a chore.

Everything began to feel like a real headache. I specifically remember one day having a pain go from the back of my neck to top of my head and I thought "oh my God! I am having an aneurysm"; to this day I don't know what it was. But I knew I was going to change everything that day. That was a defining moment for me, it was the impetus to put some fire under the situation and move forward.

Everything, even going to salsa, the thing I am most passionate about became a chore and that was because I was mentally and physically exhausted, stressed out, unable to focus, unable to concentrate and just unhappy in every way. Everything was affected, work, personal life and my energy were low.

Work had been a struggle, my manager was very inflexible and a micro manager. It became extremely difficult. I was able to manage for a while until I got home and perhaps would be better, I could balance it out, but getting extreme stress in the office and extreme stress at home, and something had to go and it was not going to be me. I felt split into fragments and was continually trying to repair myself.

I did not even sleep most of the time. I would wake up either thinking about how I had forgotten to do something at work, or oh my God – he is not even in bed anymore. He was sleeping in another room... it was always something. My mind was never still anymore.

When the day came when I decided to put some fire under his ass, excuse the expression, I did what I had to do? I would call it "the straw that broke the camel's back". I was working hard. I would leave home at 7am in the morning and walk in the house on average at 11:30pm at night with my laptop in hand.

One particular evening, I said good evening to my husband as he was watching the TV. I had this very long living room so he was on one end and I was coming through the door on the other end, I said "Hi" and he didn't even turn around. He just kind of raised his hand in a "whatever" manner, not responding. And just then, in that moment I thought, "Oh my God, he's not even acknowledging me in my own home - this is just not on."

I gave him one more chance and said "did you cook anything?" and he suddenly turned around and casually stated "I was busy today". And I said to myself, okay, I can do bad all by myself. I am not doing this anymore. "Today is the last day" - and it was.

The next morning I woke up with a vengeance. I went on the Internet, I printed a bunch of places for rent. I told him that I wanted to have a really serious conversation with him. I showed him all of the options. I explained how I had decided to rent our apartment out as of the following month and that people would be viewing it. I wanted him to move into one of the rooms I had selected and I would rent it for him for the first two months to help him out, as I could not continue like this anymore.

I took action

So for me, I made it another step forward. I took action with step 4.

Normally, the way I handle being in a stressful situation is I tend to be indifferent. The minute you begin to doubt yourself, you are unable to move forward. I could no longer be emotional about it. As I said before, I had done everything that I could have done before to save the marriage. At any point if he had said to me "you know what this is crazy, I want to work this out". I am sure I would have stopped, but the train was moving so I kept moving with it.

The train was moving - we both moved out

Initially, he refused to move out. He said he was not going anywhere. So that was the only way for him to move if I offered him an opportunity and I paid for the opportunity for him to move. That was the only way to get him out.

Emotionally, I did that too. I moved out of the marriage and also I wanted to move out of that negative energy that was in our home. I could have found a roommate, but I just could not see being in place once full of love and harmony which was now devoid of that and full of negativity, I literally wanted to shower myself clean and I just wanted to start fresh and get rid of all of that bad energy. I completely changed the environment.

I moved from the dark to being in the light by making some serious choices and changes. Albeit, now I had to make a huge life change. Within six months I moved out, I quit my job and I left the country.

These were all big and bold moves that were huge. I am not sure that I thought about what was going to happen when I moved back to London, which is where I went after leaving New York.

When I arrived back in the UK I said to myself, "okay here I am, what should I do now?" It sounded good on paper. I had not really thought about the other end of it. It was more about just getting out of the situation.

I have written a story in an anthology, where I talk about my dilemma. I talk about feeling invisible and needing to breathe air, because I was suffocating in the marriage. I felt suffocated in the relationship and I think once I moved to London it was the first time I felt I could breathe again. It was just like *Tony Morrison's* book "*Waiting to Exhale.*" I was able to inhale and exhale again for the first time in ages and it felt really good. I really did not know where I was going, but it couldn't be any worse than where I was coming from.

So you can see how taking a step-by-step approach helped me take a gigantic step. People still ask me now, how did I know when was the right time and to be perfectly honest, I didn't know it was. What I did know was the universe whispering to me to do it, but I didn't recognize it as that I didn't call it that. I just knew I was a great woman, I didn't know I was also a great manifester. I knew I could manifest things really well. Not necessarily easily, but if I decide to do something it usually comes to fruition.

I didn't know then what I know now. I didn't understand the power that I had, to alter and change or the ability to redirect my life as necessary. I did what came very naturally to me, so that's what I did.

It was very quick, within six months I had completely changed my life around or less than six months actually. For me it didn't really feel that quick, it felt like a lifetime. Because I had been thinking about it for a long time, for some two years. I had been planning to leave him, at least in my head, but I wanted, as I said going back to being in the position that I could say I have done everything I could do and there is nothing more I can do now. So I was comfortable and I believe I had no regrets and no sorrow and only comfort in my heart that I did the right thing.

Eventually I found the strength that I didn't know I possessed

Eventually I found strength that I didn't really know I possessed and I was happy for it. I realized I am really a strong individual and I really believe that I recognized I was listening to my intuition, but this time I was really tuned in and recalibrating when things felt wrong.

I realized that one of my greatest strengths is manifesting and prior to this I had not recognized that. Energy has always been something that is a big part of me. Something I didn't really understand and I just knew that I had used it when necessary. I didn't know what to call it, I didn't know what it was.

The Universe wants it for me

I learned that tapping into that energy and power I really trusted and believed in was important. Understanding I was manifesting what was happening because the Universe wants it for me, knowing, acknowledging and submitting to what is before me.

When it is the right situation, the universe lines up all the right things for you, because this is what is meant to happen. The Universe will never send you in the wrong direction. But I came to learn and understand that better down the road.

I kept tools and techniques that I have learned to keep with me when I move from the dark place to the lighter place and they are the same tools and techniques I use to balance myself in the place where I now stand - harmony. They are the same tools and techniques I use to manifest everything thing I desire as and when I desire it.

One of the most important things for me is meditating. It's really important, even if you are just breathing deeply, continuing to practice the practice, to become better at it is to become consistent. The biggest challenge while learning to meditate for me has been to get my mind to stop having conversations that were running around 24/7 in my head. I just needed to quieten the noise and meditating just gives you silence in a way I never experienced before. I use that as one of my techniques.

I have coaching sessions with my amazing coach who is truly amazing! I'm not just saying that. She helps me to tune into what I already know and what I know to be true and that's been a tremendous help. Being true to what really makes me happy is an important desire for me, which I discuss in one of my forthcoming books.

One of the things that has always been a passion of mine is salsa dancing. For some reason the minute I hear that music and the minute I start dancing, it is as if nothing else exists. Just myself, the person I am dancing with and the music. It could be the most crowded room, but it suddenly feels empty in a good way.

The feeling is of Fred Astaire and Ginger Rogers dancing around without a care in the world. It is as if you become five years old again and you are just playful and joyful and having no inhibitions. You are not fearful, you are fearless and you can do anything your mind decides you want it to do because you are only in a "can do" mode.

Wow, that's impressive

I tend to have a very positive attitude as a rule. I spend a good part of my life staying away from negative people and negative attitudes.

I have friends and family members that the minute you say something positive they will come up with ten negatives so I have learned to instead of saying I am thinking about doing this, so they can give you a reason as to why you shouldn't do it, I just say something like did I tell you I am doing this next week or did I tell you I did that last week and what can I say it's been done. Then all of a sudden they say wow, that's impressive – and it is isn't it? This is what I do!

As a rule, it is important that you make sure you are in a positive environment all the time. It's really, really important, I can't stress that enough.

Sometimes people around you are in a negative space. I do my best to understand if what you see is really what you get? When I say this I mean is this person really unhappy because they are bringing unhappiness in their life into the workspace or into their environment. It just oozes out of their pores because they are miserable or are they generally an unhappy person and it doesn't matter what you do for them they will never change because that's their disposition and that's who they want to be. They must enjoy being in that space. I try hard not to discount people immediately, but if I feel negative energy I can walk in a room and feel it not having met the person and not spoken to them. I just say okay the negative energy is coming from the right, so I am going to the left and I don't indulge. I don't entertain it. It's just that simple. Or, when I am in a situation, for example, when I am at work, at an event or if at a party, once I am around that type of energy I can become uncomfortable if I am in a situation where it's not easy to get away. I am just pleasant and then I just excuse myself. I just move away. I don't take it on.

Some people do take them on. Some people absorb other people's negative energy, but I don't. I make a point of not absorbing negative I deflect it.

There are reasons I choose not to absorb it. There is definitely a negative effect of absorbing both physically and mentally. I mean, it's just you take on someone else's bad energy and it brings you down. It doesn't do anything positive for you. It's draining; I call these people energy suckers. I mean some people I have met in general who, when you are around them, I feel drained in their presence. For me, I've got to go. I can't take it on. Even physically feel them sucking the life out of me. As I make a point of keeping negative people at arm's length.

Being around positive people is paramount. The effect is so wonderful because you can bounce ideas, energy, thoughts and feelings of that person and it's great because you are on the same vibe. You enhance each other, you bring some light to them, they bring some light to you. It's such a wonderful place to be.

Having made these tweaks my life has now become physically and emotionally changed. I have made a total 90-degree turnaround. I am even in a better place than I was before. Now I am very comfortable with the person I am. I have made no excuses how I live my life, nor will I.

I have lived my life in the way I have always wanted, but I had not really grasped who I was. I don't think I claimed the power of my greatness; I use that word, my own "greatness" without arrogance. Because I know I not am arrogant and I am confident and comfortable with all of these attributes. When one is really happy in their life, others think it can't be, that nothing can be that wonderful, but it depends on your definition of greatness, or your definition of wonderfulness. I am really happy with the person I am, but I love the person I have evolved into so I am learning more and more about me every day and I am loving everything, I see - it's really good.

I have achieved a lot in a short space of time along with discovering some gifts I didn't know I had. I am doing so much, creating products and services. Let me tell you a little bit about what has allowed me to achieve this.

I would say that being a coach is an amazing experience. There is power in coaching, it's not the same as mentoring, it's another individual, allowing you to answer the questions you already know, but bringing them to the forefront and then you examine them and then act on them. What happens is where were these ideas that we really want to do? But then someone says to you "you can't do that because x, y or z". Or you step in your own way and you don't make it happen. "Oh I really would love to go here, but I can't afford it, how can I get there? Who is going to help me? I can't do it on my own." You come up with all these excuses. So coaching helps you to realize that as my father used to say *you are your own worst enemy.* If you step up to the challenge, and if you really desire something you can make it happen. You have to really want it and be willing to make the sacrifice, which is required to make it happen. Great things don't really happen with you laying around and waiting for things to fall into it your lap it just doesn't happen that way. You have to do the work. If you are committed to doing the work you will see the change.

As the first Joy Spot Practitioner/Relationship Coach, and Author, I have come a long way, and there were a few reasons why I decided to become a coach.

It began really because pretty much everybody and their grandmother, I know would call me for advice. They would say I used to do this thing or that I was a really nice person, because I am open, and they feel very comfortable talking to me and I like that. Not only am I open and a good listener, but I tend to love hearing everyone's business. But I don't give it out. Then I would know everyone would stop sharing. I like that, people trust me and are comfortable sharing with me.

It started from that perspective. I used to think – ooh if only that person knew what that person thinks of that person! I would say this in my mind. But then people asked me really big life questions and it's really kicked off in its formative stage when I left my husband.

When I left him I would say to people openly, as I am that sort of person, "yeah, yeah I left my husband. It's the best thing I have ever done".

People would email me, call me or whisper to me in a situation, "Oh my God, what did you do, would you teach me how to do it?" I was shocked because the people I thought were perfectly happy weren't. And were having a way better relationship than me, were coming to me asking me for advice. Saying "I want to know the secret - how did you leave?" I began to realize that maybe I had something there, a gift where I could share experiences, as it was very natural it wasn't forced, with other people that were in a similar dilemma.

As I said before, I have always been a caretaker. It is a natural transition to help take care of other people in a different way from a professional perspective.

The impetus to do it came from having dialogues with people about what was going on in my life and I think just being honest about my story and experience. It made people relate and connect because it wasn't just me talking theoretically from documentation. It was more a case of this is my life experience and I am sharing it with you so you feel comfortable to have the ability to share yours with me and we are on the same page, I am no different than you are.

I started my having a relationship with myself first

I started by having a relationship with myself first. Let's talk about the relationship with myself because obviously you can tell I am expressive, happy and a magnificent person. So I shall tell you how I came to be that person again from an awful place.

It's getting to know myself all over again, and it was very interesting because I remember moving back to England and calling my best friend and saying to her I think I am depressed and she said "don't be silly you are not depressed what are you talking about", I said "no, I really think I am depressed I never experienced depression but I think this must be it" and she asked "oh why are you so depressed" and I said "I sit and watch soap operas every night. I mean I use to be in New York in a theatre, going out to dinner, night clubs, galas, etc. and here I am sitting on my flat mate's couch watching soap operas" and she said "may be that's what you are meant to be doing right now, maybe you are just meant to sit still and be one with yourself!"

I thought, okay, my friend is crazy now, okay, she really doesn't know what she is talking about and I am not having any more conversations with her because she has given me some weird advice.

That conversation resonated with me and stayed in the back of my mind and I thought what if I just succumb to this, what if just go with the flow, what if I just watch TV and one day I won't really want to watch any more. What if I just **be** in the moment, **be** in the now and go with what seems right.

What my gut was telling me, even though my head was saying this is not what we do, we don't lay on the couch and watch TV we are reading. But what in essence was happening, I was clearing my mind and clearing the pathway. I was moving away from all the negativity that I had experienced and I was almost sort of flushing it out and reconnecting with me. I think, I know that the journey really became serious when I went to India I guess almost three years ago. Where I practised yoga twice a day at sunrise and sunset for ten days and I learned how to begin to meditate and I realized, okay I am on a different path I am back on the path of me! We have to be happy within ourselves otherwise you can't be happy with someone else or something else - as it all starts within!

Although, I have written a book; The Joy Spot, Sex, Love and Men and there are four things in the book that are important to me. In my book, I talk a lot about loving yourself, it is a big part of the book. Following along my journey you may be beginning to question and to wonder if I began to slowly start falling in love with myself again or fall out of love with myself further.

I always believed I was worthy and still do

I don't believe I ever fell out of love with myself because if I had fallen out love with myself it would have been really difficult to find love again. I know what happened to me was love on mute. I never stopped loving myself because I believe I had to be strong in and with love in order to go forward for me to have the strength to leave my situation. And I probably owe that to my love of self. I always believed I was worthy and still do.

I soon came to terms with the fact that I knew I loved myself more than I loved this relationship. And loving myself more had to come back to the forefront. My self-love became so quiet that it was almost on mute and I had to bring that vibration out again I had to come back to the forefront and be heard and I couldn't hear myself.

The one key thing I learned on that journey was probably just how important I was. How lost I was by becoming someone else. I was busy loving someone else I was busy doing for everybody else but myself and I think a lot of women who are married and who have children are guilty of that. We focus on loving everybody else, we put everybody else as the priority and if we don't and we choose to love ourselves, we either guilt ourselves, or we are made to feel guilty. I used to go to the spa every month religiously every other week, to get my hair done and do nails, because these are the things that made me feel good. And feeling good resulted in my husband, loving me more finding me sexier, etc. and all that went out the window. I wasn't loving me anymore wasn't doing the things that made me feel good and showed me how good I felt, so I think that the key thing was just that.

There are five steps that I want to share with my readers that would help with being in a dark place and moving to a place of joy and harmony.

Step 1

 Recognizing that there is an issue by moving out of denial. This first step is powerful and probably the hardest step to take.

Step 2

Is being honest with yourself. You have to ask yourself honest questions, which most people don't want to do let alone hear the answers. My rule of thumb has always been "don't ask the questions, if you really don't want to hear the answers" as you have to be really honest with yourself and look at what's really going on. As Michael Jackson said – "I'm starting with the Man in the Mirror."

Step 3

In the coaching world, the exercise, wheel of life is a really great tool. It is based on looking at different areas of your life and really need to look at which path is really important to you by rating them, figuring out what's the priority and what's not the priority. Prioritizing this key if use in your life or things that you believe to be issues and then focus on where your happiness lies on them. If number one is the most important thing that you desire most that's the first thing that you need to action on and then you want to break that down further and look at that really closely and start figuring out how you can work through the things that you consider the issues to resolve or get you to that place of desire.

Step 4

Number one is awareness that you are unhappy. That's not always easy. Once you have decided that you are going to take action, then its figuring out what that will be, so is it coaching, is it therapy is it a big action or a small action? It may be lots of small actions to get to a bigger place. That would depend on whom and where the individual really is? What's the issue you are trying to confront? And do you need to make some changes with the new self as opposed trying to try to make changes around somebody else.

Step 5 - After you have gone into the zone then you have to apply the change moving forward with action and decision, in order to do whatever is necessary next.

The gift is in knowing and learning how to change something. Or whilst deciding to make a change, actually applying the idea and then keep moving forward in the meanwhile.

As a reminder, like everyone, once in a while we get stuck we tend to plateau. It's easy to fall off the wagon, for want of a better term, but get back to basics. It's not easy. The most effective thing you can do is to is to stop and breath, look around and surmise where you really are and then move forward. Then, continue from where you are. Don't go into panic mode and say this isn't working so I am going to stop here. Instead, continually work through your plan of trying to become a better you.

Essentially, what I am saying is always trust your instinct, I always do. It will enlighten you and give you divine happiness.

About Michelle Lowe

Michelle Lowe aka *Divalowe* is *The World's only Relationship Event Planner Coach*, advising and training women and men over 35 on understanding, appreciating and navigating through the peaks and valleys of finding love. **Soon to be released books:-** Meandering Mind Sports in the 21st Century and Men, Love, Joy and Sex.

Website: www.joyspotseries.squarespace.com

Email: michelle@yolobespoke.com

Location: New York, USA/London, UK

Notes & Ideas:

"You have power over your mind – not outside events. Realise this, and you will find strength"

Marcus Aurelius

Soul Music

By Kristina Mendez-Matejova

I love music. I adore all its forms, styles and sounds. I can honestly say that there is at least one musical piece in every genre that I enjoy. I cannot get enough of music; its potential that allows every human being to express their souls in their beautiful individuality, as well as bring important messages to us from the infinite pool of wisdom also known as collective consciousness.

Music stirs life within me and brings it to the surface with a force that if not released would burn me to dust. When I am touched by music in this way, I cannot help but let it flow out of me. Most of the time I dance. I allow the tones to flow through me and move me like a master puppeteer. I feel alive, present and full of infinite joy when I dance. I do not possess any exceptional talent in dance or special abilities in bodily movements. I am not sure what my dancing looks like to the outside world, but it feels amazing to me. I enter a zone where nothing else matters apart from the flow of music at that particular moment in space and time.

I have also been known to attempt to let the music flow through my fingers on a guitar. I find the subtle vibration of the wood and strings under my hands very appealing. Although I can barely play one simple piece of music and the first few bars of another, I have imposed my 'art' onto my friends and family with a jolly smile on my face and pride of a five-year old in my heart.

Nothing gets through the invisible and invincible blockage

There are times when I am alone in silence and my soul is bursting into a song. I can hear and feel it building up within me, my chest swelling with breath, ready to be released from the bottom of my belly to allow the song flow into the world. I feel the pressure building, the expectant excitement, the apprehended joy as I am about to burst into a song of my being. I open my mouth and... And nothing happens... My body deflates, disappointment rushes over me like a cold shower.

The pressure has built up in my throat, but nothing gets through the invisible and invincible blockage. There is no sound, not even a croak or hoarse whisper, just heavy silence. Not the beautiful intentional silence pregnant with all the possibilities of creation, but the empty void in the absence of what should have been. All the pleasure and joy that was to come has dissipated and left me hanging, standing alone with my mouth open, feeling numb and empty. It happened again.

My music was shut down by my wounded heart. The fear of rejection, judgement and failure is stronger than the desire to express my soul's symphony. You might wonder why am I scared of judgement and rejection when I am alone with no witnesses to my stumbling performance. The thing is, my mind is my harshest critic. It has assimilated all those words I'd been told as a child, turned them into deep-seated beliefs and now puts every syllable I utter under such scrutiny that the FBI should hire it.

I am not in possession of a natural singing talent to grant a career in the music industry and that is not where my passion lies either, but I do have a voice; surely that is enough to make some kind of music? My mind does not think so.

I was brought up by highly critical parents in a school system that was only interested in uniform results as opposed to nurturing the individual, building on their strengths and supporting them in their weaker subjects. My mother is very musical. She sings beautifully and used to play guitar to accompany her voice. I loved listening to her songs at bedtimes and by the fire in the summer evenings. The melodies and words used to stir a little fire within me that bubbled up to the surface accompanied by a burning desire to join her and share this amazing music with her.

I was about five, perhaps six with no former musical education and so I sang only as well as I knew how. I could hear that my notes did not match my mother's, but I did not know how to correct that. Instead of teaching me or at least gently correcting me, my mother used to tell me to stop singing. She would say that I howled like a wolf and that it was hurting her ears. I certainly did not wish to hurt my mother's ears, so I stopped immediately. I never questioned her authority on this. I formed a belief that if I was able to learn, she'd teach me. The fact that she didn't teach me, therefore meant that I was a lost case and could never learn how to sing. And so I didn't. I absolutely believed I could not sing at all, never could and there was no point in trying.

As a result, I'd developed a very strange relationship with music. I loved listening to music and knew a fair amount of it in theory, but I hated when I was requested to create or express music myself.

Where I grew up, the musical education in primary school consisted of having to learn songs assigned by the teacher and then singing those in front of the class. You'd then get verbally appraised by the teacher and marked in the sight of and hearing about everyone else.

I remember vividly one particular occasion of such class. I was about seven and at that time I was a quiet, shy and withdrawn child. My teacher called me to the front and asked me to sing my assigned song. I shook like a leaf. I could not bring myself to face the children that were all staring at me expectantly, so I angled myself in a way that only allowed me to see my teacher. I took a deep breath in to steady myself, but that did not really help as all I could think of was my mother's voice telling me to stop howling. The teacher impatiently rapped her fingernails on the desk. As I sang as best as I could. I was able to hear that it was not pitch perfect, the bum notes grating on my ears just as much as everyone else's. I felt the heat in my cheeks and my voice disappearing into a distant whisper. I looked up at the stern face of my teacher. "You should not be singing in public, really. You sound like you are pulling a cat's tail. I'll mark you three as you at least got the lyrics right."

I heard the sniggers and suppressed laughter from the class, but I dared not look at their faces. With my tear filled eyes looking down I made my way back to my desk and sat down heavily, knowing that music is dead within me, that I'd never be able to feel the joy of breaking into a song, I now knew I completely lacked the ability to do so.

As a result of these experiences in my early childhood, I stopped singing completely. Not even the shower walls would hear my voice rising in tune. If I found myself in a social situation where singing in a group would be required, I'd just mouth the words. Looking back, I realise how much those experiences affected my life.

I became a very quiet, withdrawn child, my voice barely a whisper. I avoided being a centre of attention in a group, but demanded it with my loved ones. I had a tendency to lash out or sulk a lot, always feeling the victim of others or life in general.

I have always felt that I had something to offer the world, despite what my parents or teachers said. I was not sure what it was or how I would share it, but I felt I was meant to communicate with and to others who I am in order to show them who they are. I could not put it in these words at the time, but I knew that by withdrawing myself I went against my very nature.
As I grew older, I found myself unable to speak in front of groups of people to or to scream at will. My expressions of intense joy, pleasure, anger and frustration were all silent. If I tried to use my vocal chords, the sound would get stuck in my throat and nothing would come. After a while, I just accepted that this was me, this was how I was. Kristina cannot and does not sing. End of story.

But it was not meant to be the end of my story, as I realised three years ago. I met a wonderful man. A man of many talents amongst which was the ability to play multiple instruments, to compose, write and produce music, as well as singing and dancing. If there was a God of music, he'd take the perfect form of this man. He put a guitar in my hands and showed me that I too have music within me, he challenged me and coaxed me out of my soundless cave, he even gave me a guitar and encouraged me to sing the sounds while playing.

When I held the guitar in my hands and played a few simple chords, something within me had stirred that I could no longer contain. I felt that the time had come to let my music out into the daylight. I was still apprehensive about using my voice, but I understood now I was not completely tone deaf and I was able to reproduce a melody.

The next day, I got an email from GroupOn offering me a discount for three singing lessons. My heart skipped a beat. I knew this was it. I bought the voucher without hesitation and contacted the teacher straight away.

Nevena was a classically trained singer with an amazing voice and lots of experience in performing as well as teaching. At the end of our first session, I was able to get through half of a song without cringing at the horrible sounds coming out of my mouth. After all the warm ups and exercises at the beginning of the session, I managed to gain enough control of my voice to produce a recognisable melody that was reasonably pleasant to the ear.

With each session my confidence and ability grew. I started to practice at home, sing in the shower, record myself and even dared to sing in front of my best friend. This was nerve wracking to start with, but each time I sang I grew more and more comfortable with my voice and musicality.

I still hit plenty of bum notes and I am far from being a confident performer, but I am able to sing to myself, to allow my voice to project when singing in a group and even dared to attend a work's social at a Karaoke bar, where I performed one solo song after warming up by singing with others. I actually ended up singing all night and really enjoyed the experience.

I've noticed that since then my stage confidence has improved over all. I find it much easier now to speak in public in front of an audience, but I know my work here is not done yet. There is still lots of fear involved and I am unable to scream at will.

Fortunately, I have surrounded myself with amazing, supportive people who are helping me along the way, while I use different therapies to get better longer lasting results. I am proud of how far I have come and I am really happy that I can now enjoy singing to my little nephews without worrying that I'd scar them for life. I have been complimented on my public speaking skills, which is a truly unexpected side effect of letting my song flow. I have found a new ability to connect to my heart and through it to the collective consciousness while allowing the information to flow through me without judgement or need to control it. Because of this phenomenon

I constantly find myself amazed at what is coming out of my mouth with such passion and confidence.

Often, what I say, I hear for the first time also and I learn as I speak. I find that I do not need to learn speeches by heart, I just need to allow the speech to flow from my heart. I've noticed the same flow with writing. As I type, new ideas that had never occurred to me before develop in front my eyes. All I must do is to take a deep breath, connect to my heart, and let go of any preconceived ideas of the outcome; then miracles happen. All this has come to me only after I allowed my music into the outside world.

Now, I feel much more connected to my heart, soul and others. My communication style has improved enormously, I am much more confident, my voice is steady and my demeanour is calmer and softer. With the ability to express myself from my core, came this quiet confidence with who I am and faith in the value of what I have to say. Does that mean that I would stand up on a stage and sing to thousands of people? No. Absobloodylutely not. However, I am now able to entertain the idea of speaking on a stage in front of hundreds of people. I consider this a huge step up from not being able to sing to myself in a bathroom or ask a stranger for directions.

I believe that we can all sing even if we are not able to follow or copy someone else's melody. Who says that music has to sound one way or another? Make your own music, your own songs, and release them from your heart into the big wide world. Somewhere out there is someone who needs to hear it. Let the wind carry it forth, let it go without worrying about its destination. Allow your soul to soar to the skies with the song. Feel your breath, your love, expand and fill you up letting the aliveness flow through you, cleansing you of all the stuckness, fear and numbness, letting the light in, brightening up the darkness within. Music is an integral part of humanity. By allowing your music to flow through you and into the world, you are reconnecting with yourself, your deepest, darkest parts as well as with the eternal light of your soul, you are reconnecting with the nature, universe, God and embracing your true self, your true voice.

Each song is an important part of the life's symphony. The masterpiece cannot be complete without your song. It cannot be complete without mine either, so let me leave you with a song on your lips and melody in your heart and let's keep creating the most beautiful symphony of them all, together.

Through this journey, I have come to understand that we all have a voice, we all have something to say and we all can sing. We might not produce melodies pleasing to others, but as long as we are not forcing our music onto others, that's our own business.

Everyone is capable of creating and expressing a melody that is pleasing to them and that's what matters. I learned that holding the music in you is destructive in the long term as it limits all creativity and aliveness, stopping us from living to our full potential. I also realised, how important it is to address any limiting beliefs we might have acquired in our childhood and adolescence, as they can often run our lives through our subconscious, meaning that we are not in the driver's seat and we are not even aware of it, happily stirring the wheel that is not connected to the rest of the vehicle and wondering why we end up going in the wrong direction despite our best and often frenzied efforts to avoid a collision.

We think we are in control, when all the while, our lives are on an autopilot. Becoming aware of our patterns and core beliefs and changing those that are no longer helpful (this often requires professional assistance) is probably the most important step on our journey towards self-fulfillment and reaching our dreams.

If you find yourself in the same boat, if you feel unable to sing, dance, speak, or express yourself fully in the presence of others, then I hope these few words will serve as an encouragement and inspiration, showing you that you too can do anything that makes your heart sing, no matter what anyone else says.

First of all, become aware of the push/pull feeling that is a telltale sign you have limiting beliefs about a way of expressing yourself, that you are currently suppressing. For example, when I was at a karaoke with friends, I really longed to join them and sing, but my mind completely pushed that feeling down and shut me up, so I never did, simply telling them and myself that I don't sing.

This might not apply to singing for you; perhaps you were led to believe that you cannot draw, dance, swim, run, or whatever. If you were, and think, "Oh, I wish I could do that." Then it is a pretty safe bet that this is your heart's desire, but your mind is telling you that you are not enough this or that.

Not everyone will be the next Dalí, Darcy Bussel or Beyonce just because they like to paint, dance or sing. Following your heart is not about the end result or success, it is about enjoying the process. That is what will bring you lasting fulfilment. If you only feel fulfilled when you achieve something, that feeling will be sparse. However, if you are fulfilled by simply doing something no matter how well, that feeling can be everlasting.

Once you become aware of your limiting beliefs, find a suitable professional therapist and work on removing those. As you do this, it'll become easier to follow the next step, do what brings you joy, no matter how well or badly you think you do it.

Of course you can also adjust your perception by realising that if there is no judgement, there is no bad or good, better or worse, just different, unique. Then, take it a step further and share your joy, invite others to join you, create a space for others to express their souls without the fear of judgement or rejection.

Suddenly you look back and realise you have become a teacher, in the true sense of the word. You have given the world what it really needed, your true self.

About Kristina Mendez-Matejova

Kristina Mendez-Matejova is a Massage Therapist and an Aromatherapist. She believes in the capacity of all living organisms to heal themselves as well as each other. Kristina has always felt a calling to assist people in the process of healing. She believes that massage is a great medium for self-healing and improving self-awareness.

Website: www.kmmserenitytherapies.co.uk

Facebook: www.facebook.com/kmmserenitytherapies

Location: London, UK

Notes & Ideas:

"Let Your Heart Sing"

Even the darkest clouds have silver linings

By Joumana Nasr

The toughest challenge I went through that had me living in complete dissonance has to be the depression I went through back in 2009.

You see, at the end of 2008, my sister passed away suddenly and she passed away at a time when I was already physically, mentally and emotionally exhausted. I had gone through three years of major, major life changes: everything from moving countries, moving cities, my daughter going away to college, my son starting high school, a complete house remodel in 7 weeks, to the holiday season and a few things in between. So I was exhausted and I knew that I was exhausted, and I was stressed out. Yet I just kept pushing myself, saying to myself things like: "I just need to get this one more thing done and then I'll take care of myself", "it's almost over". But I never got to the taking care of myself part because just before I could, my sister passed away at the end of 2008, and it was like the straw that broke the camel's back.

At the time, I just thought it was grief. The thought that it may be depression never even crossed my mind because I was always the strong one. I was known in my family as the strong one, very level headed, feet firmly planted on the ground. So, I just thought it was a normal part of the grieving process. I definitely knew that I was exhausted, so I thought I just needed to give it time. It would pass. I would get through it. It's the grieving process. And it hit me hard because it was my sister and I was extremely close to her because she was the oldest child in my family and I was the youngest. There was a 20-year age difference between us. When I'd go shopping with my mom and my sister, people would think I was with my mom and my grandmother.

She was my sister, she was my mother, she was my friend. Her loss was a huge blow for me and an even bigger shock. And because my body was so exhausted already, it just basically shut down. It all caught up with me and I was drowning.

First of all, I had no energy. I couldn't get out of bed in the morning. I really had to push myself. I would go through days where I would literally take my son to high school to drop him off in my pjs because I didn't have the strength to get up, take a shower, get dressed and drive him to school.

Emotionally, I was going through a lot of different emotions. I was angry. I felt guilty. Everything grated on my nerves. I couldn't turn on the TV because the sound just bothered me. It got on my nerves and overwhelmed my senses. I would dread when my family would come home just because of the noise they would make. The hustle and bustle that comes with their presence bothered me and that made me feel shame and guilt, like "how can I feel like this about them?" They are my family, the people I love the most the world in. There were no answers to that. It was just part of that whole thing that falls under depression.

In addition to that, I couldn't keep up with conversations because I just didn't have the attention span. Besides, I didn't have the energy to participate in any conversation. It's like I just didn't want to deal with anything. I was completely disconnected from things like what's for dinner, how was your day and whatever. I was unable to engage in all that.

In fact, even being with the family put so much more stress on me because I always felt like I needed to have dinner on the table, do laundry and all of that stuff and I just couldn't. I just didn't have it in me because I didn't have the strength or the energy to do it.

That was on the emotional and mental level, on the physical level, first of all I gained about 40 pounds and my body just kinda shut down. I developed food sensitivities and allergies that I never had before because my body wasn't able to digest food properly anymore. Everything either came to a standstill or was going in very slow motion. I would have a meal and then I would get heartburn or gas or would get bloated (sometimes all three) because my digestive system simply wasn't working optimally. These symptoms are not what you would directly associate with depression but they are side effects of what the body has to go through while battling depression, the sluggishness experienced during depression. For example, when your digestive system is sluggish because the depression has made everything sluggish, eating heavy foods or fried foods will cause problems because it won't get digested properly so it will just sit there and make you feel even worse physically which then makes you feel emotionally worse and it becomes a vicious circle. Even my brain became "sluggish" and slowed down, which shouldn't have come as a surprise because one thing gets affected, everything gets affected. And everything did get affected. Not all at once. It happened over time.

So the weight for example crept on a little bit at a time. It was hard to notice at first because pyjamas tend to be very forgiving, but because my energy was so depleted, I would eat thinking that would increase it just enough so I can get things done. My weight was not a priority so in a way it was neglected. My priority at the time was getting myself out of that stuckness, out of that quicksand that I found myself drowning in.

Like I've said before, I first thought it was a normal part of the grieving process and everything that came with it. But I think the turning point for me was when my cousin wanted to have a memorial mass for my sister. It was supposed to be on a Sunday and I remember that Saturday actually sitting there praying to get sick so I would have an excuse not to go to the memorial mass the next day. In my mind, this was the only acceptable way for me to get out of it at this point. Now, obviously I didn't get sick. I went to the memorial mass, but when I woke up the following Monday, I knew that this had gone beyond the grieving process because for someone to actually pray to get sick, there must be something else going on. I had seen my mom go through depression a few times in her life, so I was familiar with the symptoms and I was finally able to admit that this is actually a full blown depression and I needed to do something about it and fast.

Now for as long as I can re-remember, I was never one for pills, doctors and medications, and again because I had seen what happened with my mom, where she was taking a pill to wake up, a pill to sleep, anti-depressants, anti-anxiety, I didn't want that for myself.

The problem was I didn't know what else was out there? I had heard of Chinese herbs and alternative medicine, but I had no clue what it was all about.

Not only did I not know the details, but I also had no interest. I had been pretty healthy all my life so I never needed to educate myself or go searching for anything. Now I needed to search but I had no idea what to search for. I remember sitting there looking at my laptop wondering "what now?"

As I sat there staring at the flashing cursor in the Google search bar, I remembered that a few months before, maybe six or seven months I had found this day spa that I wanted to go to for slimming body wraps but never actually got the chance because we had opposite schedules. I also remembered reading something about healing on the website. I figured that would be a good place to start so I went to that website again. I figured that if it didn't give me the answers I was looking for at least it would give me a clue for what to search for. On the website, I had my first introduction to life coaching, energy healing and Reiki among many other things all of which I really didn't understand. So I decided to just make an appointment, but I was told the first available opening was Thursday of the following week. Back then I was not a patient person and I remember thinking "you're gonna make me wait till next week?" I made the appointment, but she must have heard the disappointment in my voice because she offered to put me on the waitlist in case of a cancellation.

I think the Universe must've also heard my disappointment because the next morning I had an email from her saying that she just got a cancellation for the following day and she asked me if I wanted it, and I was like "yes, of course I want it". I have to tell you that was the first moment of excitement I had experienced in months.

I went to see her the next day and I remember driving there and having this conversation in my head between my right brain and left brain where the left brain was saying that "what the bleep are you doing" and my right brain was saying "Well, how bad can it be? It's not like they're cutting into me or anything so just go, see what it is and see where you go from there".

I always say that for you to do something so far removed from the normal way that you do things, you have to be either open or you have to be desperate. I was definitely desperate. I was not open, I was simply desperate. I had become a spectator in my own life sitting on the sidelines watching my life playing out in front of me. It was almost as if there was this stranger now living in my body, making my decisions, interacting with my family and friends and I was anxious to "evict" and reclaim what's mine.

And to do that, here I was on my way to a healing day spa for a session for something called Reiki. I had asked her how long the session will be and was told it would run between an hour and an hour and a half. That wasn't too bad. I could do that. Well, my session was over 2 hours and a half long. It felt like my body was being lathered, washed and scrubbed but from the inside out. In addition to Reiki, she also worked with angels, she worked with crystals and as a medium, she connected with my sister, so I actually got the whole ball of wax.

Now for those of you who are not familiar with Reiki, I call it massage for the Soul. The same way that you go for a massage to work out the knots in your muscles, Reiki works out the "knots" or blocks in your energy system, the Chakra system. It helps open up your energy centers so everything works better.

That one experience was such an eye-opener for me. I walked out of that place a different person and by different person I mean I felt lighter (which I admit also had to do with the bucket of tears that I was able to release as she worked on me). But the greatest gift of that session was that I was given hope. I walked away with hope that yes, I will be able to overcome this huge challenge on my own terms.

From then on, things started to improve. And you know how it is, when you make a decision, the Universe starts to open up doors for you and clear your path. And that's what happened for me.

I realized that the most important thing I needed to do was get out of my head and silence all that sadness and sometimes negative talk about my sister, what I should've done differently, what I should've said and beating myself up for not doing it. To do that, I took on a new hobby, something that was so new for me that it would silence everything else because I needed to give it my full attention. Luckily for me, we had just bought a house that was a tear down and we fixed it all up, but the yard was still a mess so I picked up gardening as my new hobby.

I started gardening, which helped me because it occupied my mind and stopped the whole monkey mind and all the thoughts that go along with it. Plus, I was working with the earth, which is very healing, I was getting and I was out in the sun so I was getting vitamin D (which is also known as the "happiness" vitamin), and fresh air. I didn't even know at the time how important those things were. I just wanted to keep myself busy with something other than the barrage of thoughts that was going on in my head all the time. I was also getting a lot of satisfaction from seeing the results of my work and I have to admit there was a lot of pleasure in feeling productive again. The added bonus was that because I was actually tiring myself out with the work, I was sleeping much better and giving my body the chance to recuperate.

Then I saw that the adult school in my area had an introductory Reiki workshop so of course I signed up. The teacher had a Reiki Level One class the following week, so of course I signed up and the amazing thing was that there were supposed to be five students in the class that she would teach with an assistant to help but when I showed up on the first day (first of 2), I was the only one there. Did I mention that when you make a decision, the Universe starts to clear the path for you?

Things just took off from there. I felt like a little kid on Christmas morning with all these gifts around her and tearing up the wrapping paper to see what's inside.

I started learning about the "woo woo" stuff because I was still fascinated. I won a ticket in a Facebook contest, to a 3-day business retreat where I finally allowed myself to admit to myself that deep down in my core I'm a healer and that's how Precious Victories was born. I became a certified Life Coach. I learned about hypnosis and EFT. I dove deep into the Law of Attraction. I met a Lebanese-American medical intuitive and it gave me a lot of encouragement because she came from the same background as me and it was helpful to see how she had handled her family who didn't get the work that she had chosen. It's that whole left-brained thing.

Meeting her piqued my curiosity. Again, I was fascinated. To be honest with you, I truly believed that you were either born intuitive or you weren't and I didn't think I was so I was actually in awe of this woman and the work that she did. I went to see her a couple of times and she was the one who first told me that I had become gluten sensitive as well as allergic to all things dairy.

I was in awe at how accurate the information she picked up on was and how detailed. So, a couple of months later, when I received an email for an introductory class on becoming a certified Medical Intuitive, I jumped at the chance out of curiosity more than anything else because I still didn't believe I was intuitive.

On the call, the coach did a reading for one of the listeners and it was so powerful that the caller had her mind blown and at the end of the call she asked us what we thought. There was dead silence. No one spoke. I felt so uncomfortable. As an Empath (and at the time I didn't know what that meant, it was just the way I was), I picked up on all that energy and I felt like all of a sudden, I had developed a rash all over my body so of course I had to break that silence and I said that I thought what she did was amazing but I just couldn't see myself doing something like that. She asked for my permission to tap in, and I gave it.

I don't remember exactly what she said to me, but I definitely remember the way my body reacted to her words. I had tremors, I was shivering, I felt like somebody had just punched me in the gut. I had the wind knocked right out of me and just broke down in tears. This whole exchange didn't last more than a couple of minutes, but it felt like hours and at that time, I knew, intuitively, that what she was saying to me was absolutely true or I wouldn't have had such a violent reaction. After that, of course I signed up for the course and I became a Certified Medical Intuitive and now I get scan people's bodies to find any blockages, find out the operating percentages of different organs, if they have any vitamin deficiencies, and what the changes need to be made to their diet and lifestyle. It's amazing work.

I've come a long way since that period in my life where I was pushing my body beyond its limits, ignoring common sense and all the red flags. Today, I have a solid and consistent self-care routine that is a priority. Some of the tools that regularly show up on my schedule are:

- Reiki self-treatments
- Regular massages
- Walking
- Meditation
- Body scans
- Detox baths

It's been a very interesting journey which is ongoing and which has already taught me so many precious lessons among them:

- Everything happens for a reason
- If you don't listen to your body, you will get the proverbial 2x4 across the forehead. It's inevitable. Trust me on this one.
- Even the darkest cloud has a silver lining, we just need to look hard to find it
- You have the innate power to create anything you want in your life as long as you believe it's possible
- Never be afraid to ask for help
- Always remember that we're human, that means being gentle with ourselves
- We are always supported by a loving, caring and generous Universe

About Joumana Nasr

Joumana is a Medical Intuitive and Life Coach she helps women face life's toughest challenges head on, doing the required inner work and turning those challenges into life's most Precious Victories!

Website: www.preciousvictories.com

Location: Los Angeles, USA

Notes & Ideas:

"Every cloud has a silver lining"

About the Author

Denise Harris-Heigho is a well-respected business woman, Personal & Business development Transformational coach, Energy practitioner, Nutritional therapist and publisher in the UK. She managed to build 2 businesses making number one in the industry from ground zero in a short time whilst being an extraordinary mother to her 2 beautiful boys. She loves to travel with her family learning about other cultures.

A true Renaissance woman she is here to lead the new wave of people who want to combine success with spirituality, without compromising any of their values or authenticity.

Denise has a unique method to assist people grow in tune with their innate abilities, reawaken their minds to unlock the potentials within. By raising their vibration so that they live in resonance with who they truly are. Empowering them to fulfil their dream life in the shortest possible time.

She facilitates her clients to experience profound shifts so that they achieve results quickly and sustainably, bringing a wealth of experience and knowledge to her coaching sessions, book coaching and courses.

Denise lives in Surrey, UK, doing what she loves.

Website: www.resonantliving.co.uk
Email: denise@resonantliving.co.uk
Facebook: https://www.facebook.com/dharrisheigho
Twitter: @deharrisheigho